The Therapeutic Covenant

Christian Ethics, Doctor-Patient Relationships and Informed Consent

Neil G Messer

Minister of Maidenhead United Reformed Church and
Lecturer in Christian Ethics, Mansfield College, Oxford

GROVE BOOKS LIMITED
RIDLEY HALL RD CAMBRIDGE CB3 9HU

Contents

1. Introduction 3
2. Covenant 4
3. The Therapeutic Covenant 8
4. Consent in a Covenantal Context 13
5. Children, Covenants and Consent 18
6. Consent to Research 21
7. Conclusions 24

Preface

Much of this booklet originated in my dissertation for the MA in Christian Ethics of London University, and I owe heartfelt thanks to the Revd Professor Michael Banner of the Department of Theology and Religious Studies, King's College, London, for his stimulating teaching, helpful criticism and generous encouragement of my work. In the process of turning dissertation into booklet I was also greatly helped by the advice and comments of the Revd Greg Forster and the Grove Ethics Group. Any defects which remain are, of course, entirely my responsibility. My thanks are due to the Elders and members of Maidenhead United Reformed Church, who gave me generous financial support for this course of study and who continue to be most tolerant when they see my loyalties divided between pastoral responsibilities and academic pursuits. Finally, as always, I owe more than I can say to my wife Janet. Her professional interest in clinical research and her intelligent Christian faith have combined to make her a valued critic of my ideas. And all that we share together has taught me something of the meaning of covenant love.

The Cover Illustration is by Peter Ashton, after an idea by Janet Messer

Note to Subscribers: This title has been brought forward from January to replace the planned *Ethics in the Gospels* by Colin Hart, which will now be published in June 1997.

Copyright © Neil G Messer 1996

First Impression October 1996
ISSN 0951-2659
ISBN 1 85174 328 6

1
Introduction

Consider two brief stories of relationships between patients and their doctors.

A woman who has suffered for many years from a rare and serious condition has developed a close relationship with the specialist who has treated her for much of that time. It is a relationship of mutual respect, in which they have learned much together about the nature and treatment of her condition. In a phrase of Paul Ramsey's, they have become 'joint adventurers in a common cause.'[1]

A hospital doctor walks into the staff common room and tells his colleagues of the death of a patient who had agreed to act as a subject for the medical students' clinical final examinations. 'Our spleen died today!' he says.

These two stories illustrate the best and the worst of doctor-patient relationships. In the first the patient is treated with respect, as a partner who has much to bring to the relationship with her doctor. In the second the patient becomes no more than an interesting specimen: he is reduced from a man to 'our spleen.' These best and worst cases both bring home the vital importance of the doctor-patient relationship for the patient's well-being. In a changing National Health Service it remains true that such relationships lie at the centre of the health care delivered by the system. If the quality of the relationships is not right, the best system in the world will not compensate; and if the system inhibits the flourishing of good relationships between doctors and their patients, it must be judged seriously flawed.

Christian Understanding

In this booklet, I shall attempt to articulate a Christian understanding of doctor-patient relationships, rooted in the theology of *covenant*. I shall claim that, in J L Allen's words, God's nature and his actions towards human beings are 'always and everywhere expressive of covenant love,' that human beings, made in the image of God, have the capacity to enter into covenant relationships with God and one another, and that God's covenant love is the pattern on which human life and relationships should be based.[2] I shall argue that doctor, patient and others involved in the patient's care are bound together in what Allen calls a 'special covenant,' the *therapeutic covenant*; and I shall explore some of the implications of this understanding for doctor-patient relationships. I shall draw attention to *informed consent* as a key requirement of therapeutic covenant relationships and finally I shall examine two special problems in the area of consent—firstly, children and consent to treatment and secondly, consent to clinical research.

---

[1] P Ramsey, *The Patient as Person: Explorations in Medical Ethics* (New Haven: Yale, 1970) pp 5-6.
[2] J L Allen, *Love and Conflict: A Covenantal Model of Christian Ethics* (Nashville: Abingdon, 1984) pp 49-81.

Although this is an explicitly Christian theological account, I hope that it will also be of interest to non-Christian readers because, as I shall argue, the capacity to form covenants is basic to the way human beings are created. This theological view of therapeutic relationships has the capacity to teach and challenge all of us, Christian and non-Christian alike.

2
Covenant

In Christian theology, the notion of covenant has had a long, and occasionally chequered, history. It has not been immune from abuses but it nonetheless remains a central theme in the biblical tradition and a rich source for Christian theological reflection. The roots of the covenant concept, of course, lie in the story of God's people in the Old Testament. Covenant relationships in the Old Testament may be found between God and human beings, and between human beings. I shall survey these two kinds of covenant in that order.

1. God's Covenant Love

Of the covenants which God makes with human beings in the Old Testament, the one which is theologically prior to all others is the covenant of *creation*. By virtue of being our creator, God has defined his relationship with all human beings in certain ways. He has established a covenant relationship with the whole human community—the 'universal human covenant.'[3] The Sabbath is called a 'sign' of this covenant (Exodus 31.16ff). This universal human covenant is reestablished after the flood by the covenant with Noah (Genesis 9.1-17), where again God gives a 'sign of the covenant,' the rainbow.

As well as the universal covenant with the whole of humankind, God also enters into a particular covenant relationship with Israel; the story of this relationship is a dominant theme of the Old Testament. Defining events for God's covenant relationship with Israel include the covenant with Abraham and his descendants (Genesis 15 and 17), the Sinai covenant with the giving of the Law (Exodus 19-24) and the covenant with David (2 Samuel 7). God calls the covenant community of Israel into being, by an act of *election*. However, this election of Abraham and his descendants does not undermine God's commitment of himself to all people. Indeed, there is a sense in which God's call to Abraham is *for the sake* of the whole human community (cf Genesis 12.3).

---

3 Allen, *Love and Conflict*, pp 39ff.

COVENANT

The New Covenant

A recurring problem in the Old Testament is that God's people do not keep the covenant. This problem is addressed by the prophets, particularly Jeremiah. He looks forward to a 'new covenant' which God will establish with his people, which will replace the old covenant that they broke (Jeremiah 31.31-34). The Law will still have a central place in this new covenant, as it did in the old, but now people will obey it out of an inner knowledge and motivation; it will be 'written on their hearts.' Through the new covenant, God will forgive the people's sins.

According to the New Testament, Jesus has inaugurated this new covenant through his death. That is why, in the Last Supper narratives, he says, 'This cup is the new covenant in my blood' (2 Corinthians 11.25). The inauguration of the new covenant finally establishes the relationship between God and his people. As such, it is intimately bound up with Jesus' proclamation that 'the kingdom of God has drawn near'—that the fulfilment of God's purposes is at hand.

The Church and the Covenant

The church is clearly associated in a special way with the new covenant in Jesus Christ; it is made up of the people who have consciously responded to God's work in Christ and have identified themselves with the new covenant. However, the new covenant is not for the exclusive benefit of the church. The atoning work of Christ ultimately makes clear that God's covenant love is for all people. Thus, in Mark's account of the Last Supper, Jesus tells his disciples that his blood of the covenant is poured out for many (Mark 14.24) where 'many' is a Semitic idiom for 'all.'

I have referred for convenience to a succession of 'covenants' between God and human beings. However, it might be more correct, following Karl Barth, to speak of successive *expressions* of the one act of God by which he establishes his covenant with humankind, which is both revealed and fulfilled in the person and work of Jesus Christ.[4]

We can identify some characteristics of God's covenant love from the biblical narratives.[5]

Initiative

Firstly, there is a pattern of *initiative and response*. In all biblical covenants between God and human beings, the initiative is God's. These covenants are clearly not between equal parties—yet there is a certain reciprocity about them: 'You shall be my people, and I will be your God' (eg Jeremiah 11.4). God's initiative calls for a human response. Sometimes the expected response is set out in highly detailed ways, as in the law codes of the Sinai covenant (Exodus 19-24).

---

4 K Barth, *Church Dogmatics*, vol IV/1, trans G W Bromiley (Edinburgh: T and T Clark, 1956) pp 22-78.
5 The list that follows has some debts to Allen, *Love and Conflict*, pp 60-74, and to G Quell and J Behm, 'diatheke,' in G Kittel (ed), *Theological Dictionary of the New Testament*, vol II, trans G W Bromiley (Grand Rapids: Eerdmans, 1964) pp 106-134.

Commitment

Along with God's initiative goes his *commitment* of himself to the covenant; specifically, his commitment to the total well-being, or *shalom*, of his covenant partners. *Shalom*, often translated 'peace,' expresses all that is necessary for human beings to flourish as God created them to do: centrally, right relationships with God and with one another and also such good things as bodily health, long life and the meeting of one's material needs. In the New Testament, this 'peace' is seen as a promise whose fulfilment has begun with the in-breaking of God's kingdom into the world through the life, death and resurrection of Christ.

Community

Since right relationships are a vital aspect of the 'peace' or well-being to which God commits himself, *community* is another important feature of his covenant love. God's initiative in making covenants with human beings calls covenant communities into being. The most fundamental of these is the universal human covenant community, which takes its identity from God's initiative in creation. Israel in the Old Testament is another such covenant community. God's action in creating covenant communities is *inclusive* rather than exclusive; we all belong to the universal covenant community simply because we have been created human and when God creates a more specific community, he does so for the sake of all people.

Faithfulness

Related to God's self-commitment is his *faithfulness*. This is expressed by the Hebrew word *hesed*, 'steadfast love.' In his covenant with David God promises, 'I will not take my steadfast love from [your offspring]' (2 Samuel 7.15). This also suggests a *permanence* about God's covenants; God will not go back on his word and his promises will stand for ever. Thus the covenants with Noah, with Abraham and with Israel at Sinai are described as 'everlasting' or 'perpetual' covenants.

Worth

Finally, in calling a covenant community into being, God *affirms the worth* of every member of that covenant community. Each member is treated as a being who is capable of entering into a covenant relationship with God and with whom God wishes to make such a relationship. This applies first and foremost to the universal human covenant. All human beings are 'ends in themselves,' not because rational nature is in itself of absolute or unconditional value, but because God in his universal covenant with humankind has bestowed such worth upon all of us.[6]

Because God affirms the worth of each human being in this way, he shows particular concern for the weak, the vulnerable and the powerless—all those who

---

6   *Contra* I Kant, *Groundwork of the Metaphysic of Morals*, ed and trans H J Paton (London: Hutchinson, 1948) pp 90-91.

tend to be neglected or exploited by others. Thus the Psalmist writes, 'the LORD maintains the cause of the needy, and executes justice for the poor' (Psalm 140.12).

2. Human Covenant Relationships

Relationships within a covenant community are defined and constrained by the terms of the covenant around which it is built. For all human beings, the first covenant which defines our relationships with one another is *the universal human covenant*. We are all members of the same moral community because we have all been created human by God.[7] We have been made in God's image, so we have the capacity to enter into covenant relationships, with God and with one another, which reflect the characteristics of God's covenant love towards us.

Therefore all our dealings with one another should display the features of covenant relationships. We should be willing, when the need arises, to take the *initiative* in establishing relationships with others, or to *respond* to the initiatives of others. To refuse to do either of these things is to refuse to be fully human. We should be *committed* to seeking the well-being, or *shalom*, of other human beings and we should be willing to challenge and oppose whatever threatens the well-being of anyone. We should stand for *community* against any kind of excessive individualism, self-seeking or fragmentation of human society. We should promote *inclusiveness* against any tribalism, chauvinism, or alienation of any member of the human community. We should seek to be *faithful*, to be people whose commitment to our neighbours will stand the test of time and who can be depended on. We should remember the *permanence* of the human covenant community; although particular human relationships do grow, change and wither over the course of time, our obligations to our neighbour as *fellow human being* will never change, because they are established by God. Finally, as God *affirms the worth* of all members of the universal covenant, so should we. Anything that diminishes the worth of any human being, that treats anyone *merely* as a means, should be opposed.

Special Covenants

However, within the context of the universal human covenant, human beings are also capable of forming specific relationships for particular aims and purposes. Many of these specific relationships have the potential to be covenantal in character because human beings are created with the capacity to make covenants. In Allen's phrase, such relationships can be 'special covenants.'[8] Ultimately, therefore, special covenants derive their strength and identity from God's covenant love. God is involved in special human covenants as *pattern, witness* and *guardian* of the relationship. Thus, for example, in the biblical story of the covenant between David and Jonathan (1 Samuel 18.1-5 *et seq*), the covenant is made in the presence of God and is described as a 'covenant of the LORD' (20.8).

---

7   See Allen, *Love and Conflict*, pp 37 and 39-41.
8   Allen, *Love and Conflict*, pp 41ff.

Special covenants may therefore be expected to reflect the nature of God's covenant love, and to share many of the characteristics of the universal human covenant. However, they differ from the universal covenant in some ways. For example, they have limited membership; they exist to fulfil specific purposes, which may be quite limited; some may not be permanent, as God's covenants with human beings are. The particular characteristics of a special covenant will be determined by the purposes for which it exists, as well as the standard of covenant love which must underpin it.

3
The Therapeutic Covenant

In the field of medicine, a patient, a doctor and any others involved in the patient's medical care constitute just such a special covenant community: the *therapeutic covenant*. The special conditions of the therapeutic covenant are defined by the particular needs, opportunities and constraints which the patient's situation supplies. The character of the relationships within the therapeutic covenant should be determined by the standard of covenant love revealed ultimately in God's universal covenant with humankind.

Of course, no two patients or their doctors are identical, so every therapeutic covenant will be unique. However, it is possible to make some generalizations about the characteristics of therapeutic covenants.

Initiative and Response

As in all covenant relationships, there is some pattern of *initiative and response*. In one sense, the patient takes the initiative by approaching his doctor for help. But in the course of the patient's treatment and care, the doctor will frequently be the one who takes the initiative by suggesting a particular test, therapy or procedure. She is equipped to take the initiative in this sense by virtue of her specialized skill and knowledge. The patient needs someone who can take these initiatives.

However, this pattern of initiative and response is not without its dangers. If the doctor is seen as the partner who always takes the initiative in the patient's treatment, the relationship may tend towards what I shall call the 'benefactor-supplicant' model. Later in this chapter, I shall argue that this model is seriously inadequate as a standard for doctor-patient relationships. William F May suggests that to guard against it, doctors must remember their *indebtedness* to their patients and to the public: to their patients, because a doctor would not be a doctor if there were no patients; to the public, for providing them with the means and opportunity to learn their craft.[9]

The doctor as well as the patient has needs and indebtedness within the therapeutic covenant. Conversely, the patient as well as the doctor has responsibilities. In particular, he has a responsibility not to undermine the doctor's professional or personal status and worth—a point to which I shall return later. Thus, within the therapeutic covenant, there is a reciprocal structure of initiative and response, need and obligation. This is well expressed by Paul Ramsey's phrase, 'joint adventurers in a common cause.' The therapeutic covenant is an active partnership between doctor, patient and others concerned with the patient's care. However, it is not an entirely equal partnership since the doctor has particular power, and the patient particular vulnerabilities, within the covenant relationship. I shall discuss these inequalities further presently.

Commitment

The doctor accepts a *commitment*, which may be quite a demanding one, to seek the patient's well-being to the best of her ability and expertise. This commitment may extend over many years, or it may only last for a single consultation. However long or short its duration, the covenant model implies that a certain *quality* of commitment must always be present.

The doctor's commitment to the patient, I have said, may be limited in time. It is also limited in *scope* to the area of health and healing, so the doctor does not accept responsibility for every aspect of the patient's well-being. However, health and healing must not be defined too narrowly. Bodily health is not completely separable from other aspects of the patient's well-being, such as the emotional and spiritual. The doctor's training and expertise may not fully equip her to care for these aspects of her patient's well-being, but she should be ready to cooperate with others who can.

Inclusiveness

This point about the need for doctors to cooperate with others has a bearing on the kind of *inclusiveness* which might operate in a therapeutic covenant. Special covenants are unlike the universal human covenant in that they are made between specified people and are not all-inclusive. This is most important for the therapeutic covenant because a doctor, while she is treating a particular patient, must be free to be exclusively committed to *that patient*. An accident and emergency doctor treating a road-accident victim cannot allow her loyalties to be divided by the knowledge that there is a shortage of organs for transplantation.

However, it is also true that the therapeutic covenant should not be too narrowly exclusive. Within one therapeutic covenant community there may be a number of doctors, nurses and other health-care professionals who have some measure of obligation to the patient's care. They may be involved to different

---

9 W F May, *The Physician's Covenant: Images of the Healer in Medical Ethics* (Philadelphia: Westminster, 1983) pp 112-116.

extents, for varying lengths of time, from the general practitioner who is closely involved with her patient for many years, to the specialist whose involvement is limited to one brief consultation. The patient himself is also part of a web of relationships with family members, friends and others, all of which may have some bearing for good or ill on his well-being. Although in the present discussion I frequently refer to the 'doctor-patient relationship,' it should be borne in mind that I am including this wider network of carers, both professional and 'lay.'

Worth
Affirming the worth of one's covenant partner is a feature of every covenant relationship. In the therapeutic covenant, it works both ways round. Doctors must affirm, not deny, the worth of their patients. This means that the patient must not be patronized, refused information or treated merely as a passive recipient of medical treatment. Rather, her status as a 'joint adventurer in a common cause' must be acknowledged. But it is also possible for a patient to undermine rather than affirm a doctor's worth. Consider the case of a seriously ill white patient who refused to take her doctor's advice because he was black.[10] By her refusal she placed herself at great risk, but she also violated her covenantal obligations to her doctor by denying his professional expertise and personal worth.

However, covenant relationships require a special concern for the weak and the vulnerable. In the therapeutic covenant community the patient has particular needs and vulnerabilities and the doctor has corresponding power and importance. The patient may be ill and anxious about her condition; this anxiety may make it more difficult for her to think clearly about decisions relating to her care. Particularly if she is in hospital, she may be in an environment which is strange to her, where she is disoriented and feels that she has no control over what is done to her. The doctor, on the other hand, has knowledge and skill which the patient lacks and has a large measure of control over what is done to the patient. In short, the doctor often has considerable power over the patient. He therefore has a special responsibility within the therapeutic covenant to ensure that his power and the patient's vulnerability are not abused.

Faithfulness
This requirement to safeguard the interests of the vulnerable patient is related to the final feature of the therapeutic covenant: *faithfulness*. Joseph Allen writes that 'any special covenant...requires an appropriate kind of faithfulness.' The particular kind of faithfulness appropriate to the therapeutic covenant is the subject of the next chapter. Before I come to it, I shall contrast the covenantal model of therapeutic relationships with two other models which I believe to be unsatisfactory.[11]

---

10 R Faden and A Faden, 'False Belief and the Refusal of Medical Treatment,' *J Med Ethics 3*, pp 133-136 (1977).
11 In drawing these contrasts I am indebted to May, *The Physician's Covenant*, pp 116-127.

THE THERAPEUTIC COVENANT

Benefactor and Supplicant

The first is the *benefactor-supplicant model*: the doctor generously doles out help, which the needy patient gratefully receives. She should not dream of questioning the doctor; he knows what is best for her, and all that is required of her is a completely passive submission.[12]

The shortcomings of this model are obvious. It makes the doctor-patient relationship profoundly unequal, putting the doctor on a pedestal and placing all the power of the relationship in his hands. This is obviously bad for the patient, because it diminishes her status to that of a helpless supplicant. However, less obviously, as William May observes, it is also bad for the *doctor*. It encourages him to try and act as a superhuman, almost godlike being—which he patently is not. It tempts him to ignore or deny his own needs and vulnerabilities, and tends to make him forget that in some very important ways, he too is *indebted* to the community which he serves.[13]

Contract

The second model with which I wish to contrast the covenant concept is the *contractual model*, which has roots in a Kantian account of respect for persons and their autonomy. Here I must distinguish between two different, though related, senses in which the language of contract is used. The first is an *organizational* sense. There is much talk of contracts between purchasers and providers of health care following the National Health Service reforms of the past few years. The second is the description of *relationships*, such as the doctor-patient relationship, as contracts. It is with this second sense of 'contract' that I am mainly concerned, though I shall have a few remarks to make about the first.

Contract is a popular concept in the caring professions, including medicine. As a way of describing doctor-patient relationships it has obvious advantages over the benefactor-supplicant model. It sets doctor and patient on a more equal footing and enables the patient to play a more active part in making choices about his health care. It defines the rights and obligations of doctor and patient. It sets limits which help to guard against abuses of the relationship—for example, by requiring the patient's *free and informed consent* to particular clinical procedures.

However, I still believe that the contractual model is inadequate as a model of doctor-patient relationships. One of its dangers is what William May calls 'self-interested minimalism'; it encourages the doctor to do what is required by the letter of the contract, and no more. It can also carry the related danger of 'maximalism,' the tendency on the part of the doctor to perform every last procedure or intervention that can be done, regardless of its appropriateness to the patient's particular needs, for fear of being accused of negligence.

---

12 This is something of a caricature, but there does seem to be a certain amount of nostalgia in some quarters for this model. See D N Baron, 'Evidence Based Medical Ethics,' *J Med Ethics* 22 (1996) p 56 .
13 W F May, *op cit*, pp 112-116.

More seriously, the contractual model cannot articulate any deep and lasting commitment of doctors to the well-being of their patients; it makes medical care out to be a specified service provided for a specified fee and nothing more. I suspect that many doctors would not wish to restrict their patient care to a merely contractual relationship; if I am right about the covenantal context of human relationships, they certainly *should* not. Both as a description of what is at least *sometimes* the case in doctor-patient relationships, and as a statement of what *ought* to be the case, I believe that covenant gives a more satisfactory account than contract.

The Internal Market
The covenantal model also poses some questions for the first sense in which contractual language is used—the organizational sense of purchaser-provider contracts and the internal market. While therapeutic covenants operate at the level of the individual doctor-patient relationship rather than the whole health care system, the theology of covenant still provides a plumbline (cf Amos 7.7-9) against which to judge the system, in at least two ways. Firstly, no system or organization is exempt from the requirements of the universal human covenant. If, for example, a health care system is set up in such a way that patients in affluent areas receive quicker and better treatment than those in poor areas, then that structural injustice will stand condemned by the covenant principle that the worth of all should be affirmed.

Secondly, the health care system exists in order to allow therapeutic covenant relationships to flourish. One of the criteria by which any system should be judged is the extent to which it enables doctors, patients and others to establish relationships of faithfulness and commitment in which the worth of each is affirmed. If a system of purchaser-provider contracts in an internal market turns out to be conducive to such relationships, then in this respect at least, a covenantal account will give no grounds for objecting to it. If, on the other hand, the market places such pressure on hospitals that their doctors never have time to build up proper relationships with patients, or if it discourages fund-holding GPs from accepting certain classes of patient, then the covenant model will find the system wanting. I make no comment on whether this is actually the case; that must be for others who have more first-hand experience of the system to judge.

4
Consent in a Covenantal Context

1. The Importance of Consent

I now return to the question: What kind of faithfulness is appropriate to a therapeutic covenant? I suggest that a central feature of this 'appropriate kind of faithfulness' is the requirement for *free and informed consent*. In Ramsey's words, the consent requirement is 'the cardinal *canon of loyalty* joining men together in medical practice and investigation.'[14] Why is it so important?

Firstly, it has to do with *affirming the worth* of the patient. Her God-given status within the universal human covenant, and her corresponding status as a member of the special therapeutic covenant, demand that wherever possible she be involved as an active participant in decisions about her health care. That status is denied if things are done to her without or against her wishes, even 'for her own good.' The only exceptions to this principle occur when she is incapable of making such decisions by virtue of her state, condition or circumstances.

However, the consent requirement is not just about the nature of the person who is the patient; it is also about the *nature of the relationship* she has with her doctor. This is, or should be, a covenant relationship of mutual commitment and faithfulness. The mutuality of the relationship requires that the patient play a central role in making decisions about her health care.

Finally, the faithfulness of a covenant relationship requires special care for the interests of the weak and vulnerable. I have already remarked that in the therapeutic relationship, the patient has particular vulnerabilities and the doctor has particular power. A rigorous consent requirement is an important safeguard against intended or unintended abuses of the patient's vulnerability.

2. The Nature and Outworking of Consent

Consent as it currently operates in medicine is sometimes criticized for its narrow legalism and fragmented nature—a series of signatures on consent forms for a series of separate procedures.[15] This is one outcome of a purely contractual relationship between doctor and patient. However, in a covenantal context, the starting point for consent is not a legalistic contract, but a bond of loyalty and trust. Consent is part of an on-going relationship rather than a one-off legal hurdle. Decisions made about the patient's treatment should be made in the course of honest, open and free dialogue between the patient, the doctor and (where appropriate) others. The 'relational' aspect of consent is the most important.

There *is* also a necessary 'legalistic' aspect, since the consent requirement is

---

14 Ramsey, *The Patient as Person*, p 5 (his italics).
15 eg J F Childress, 'Consent,' in Macquarrie and Childress (eds), *A New Dictionary of Christian Ethics* (London: SCM, 1986) pp 121-122.

not only an expression of the covenant relationship but also a safeguard against its abuse. If it is to be an effective safeguard against abuse, it must be carefully worked out in legal and procedural ways. So consent forms must still be signed, there must be criteria for the adequate disclosure of information, and so on—but these are only the servants of the consent process which is one dimension of the whole therapeutic covenant relationship.

Varieties of Consent

James F Childress helpfully distinguishes between four different varieties of consent: *express, tacit, implied* and *presumed*.[16] *Express* consent is the 'paradigm case,' in which the patient makes a verbal, written or other statement, giving or refusing consent to a treatment. This is the variety which most naturally fits into a covenant relationship of trust, faithfulness and open and on-going dialogue. Apart from the exceptions which I shall discuss below, it is hard to see when or why express consent should *not* be sought.

Tacit consent is expressed by the failure to dissent. It is a popular (though controversial) concept in political theory, but it is hard to see its usefulness in a therapeutic covenant relationship. A relationship of open dialogue and communication sits most easily with express rather than tacit consent, and given the doctor's position of power, there is a danger of her *assuming* tacit consent when it has not been given.

Implied consent is inferred from the patient's decisions or actions. If a patient consents to a medical examination, her specific consent to a particular test may be inferred from her general consent to the examination as a whole. If an accident victim walks into a casualty department before collapsing, his action in entering the department can be taken to imply his consent to any necessary treatment.

In a covenantal context, implied consent does have a limited place. It may apply in emergency situations. It is also relevant in the day-to-day relationship between doctor and patient, since it would be quite impractical for the doctor to obtain a specific express consent for everything he does for his patient. However, in cases of doubt, the doctor should err on the side of express consent. For example, he may often infer consent to routine tests, but should seek the patient's express consent to tests whose results might have a profound emotional impact, such as a test for HIV infection.

Presumed consent is an assumption about the decision a person would make if she were capable of consenting. It is the farthest variety from the paradigm of express consent. Like implied consent, it has a role in emergency situations, when the patient may be incapable of giving informed consent and when, in any case, valuable time would be lost in seeking it. It may also have a role in the giving of proxy consent on behalf of children and incapacitated adults. Apart from these two situations, I can see no place for it in a therapeutic covenant relationship.

---

16 J F Childress, *Who Should Decide? Paternalism in Health Care* (Oxford: University Press, 1982) pp 80-87.

Free and Informed?

It is sometimes said that the informed consent requirement is impractical or even impossible; the patient cannot be fully informed of the nature of the proposed clinical procedures, their risks, benefits and so on, because this information is highly technical and difficult for the non-specialist to grasp. In some cases, even the doctor is unable to predict all the risks or possible consequences of a procedure, so he cannot inform the patient fully. There may also be hidden motivations and pressures operating on the patient which cast doubt on his true *freedom* in giving consent. However, as Ramsey has pointed out, the same objections could apply to almost any important decision. It is mistaken to use the limits of freedom and information as a *reductio ad absurdum* argument against the consent requirement as such. It is sufficient if the patient's consent is 'reasonably free and adequately informed.'[17]

Is it possible to define more precisely what constitutes 'reasonably free and adequately informed' consent? I shall consider the two standards, of reasonable freedom and adequate information, in turn.

Reasonably Free

Some violations of the standard of reasonable freedom are obvious and clearcut. For example, the threat of force and other forms of duress render consent invalid. However, in a clinical environment, it may sometimes be less obvious whether consent is freely given. Many factors may inhibit the patient's freedom—the clouding effect of pain or disease on his judgment, his anxiety about his future life and health and the well-being of his dependants, or elements of dependency in his relationship with his doctor. Edmund Pellegrino describes the experience of 'concealed coercion' in the doctor-patient relationship.[18] He is particularly concerned with concealed coercion in clinical research, but it is also a danger in therapy. For example, a patient who has just learned that she is seriously ill might feel desperate enough to consent to an extremely risky or painful course of treatment which she could later come to regret. Doctors, in seeking the patient's consent, must be alert to these dangers.

Adequately Informed

There is much interest in legal and moral criteria of adequately informed consent. Beauchamp and Childress discuss three: the professional practice standard; the reasonable person standard; and the subjective standard.[19] By the *professional practice* standard, adequate disclosure of information is defined as the level of disclosure which most doctors would offer. The *reasonable person* standard defines

---

17 Ramsey, *The Patient as Person*, p 3.
18 E Pellegrino, 'The Necessity, Promise and Dangers of Human Experimentation,' in S E Lammers and A Verhey (eds), *On Moral Medicine: Theological Perspectives in Medical Ethics* (Grand Rapids: Eerdmans, 1987) pp 599-610.
19 T L Beauchamp and J F Childress, *Principles of Biomedical Ethics* (Oxford: University Press, 4th edition, 1994) pp 146-150.

adequate disclosure as disclosure of all the information which a reasonable person would consider necessary in making an informed decision. The *subjective standard* requires that in any particular consent situation the yardstick should not be the needs of an imaginary 'reasonable person' but those of the *actual* person who is the patient.

None of these three standards is completely adequate, as Beauchamp and Childress acknowledge. This is certainly true from a covenantal standpoint. A therapeutic covenant relationship requires that the disclosure of information be set in a wider context—that of *teaching*. In William F May's words, 'Among several images one could use to describe the healer, the covenantal image alone demands that healers teach their patients.'[20] The adequate disclosure of information in seeking consent is only one dimension of a doctor's commitment to teach her patient how to achieve and maintain the best health that he can.

Past and Present

As Childress has pointed out, a person's consent is not just a snapshot of an instant of time.[21] A patient may express opposite wishes or consents at different times, and those who care for her may have to choose which of her expressed decisions to respect and which to overrule. Childress treats the decision between the patient's past and present wishes as an issue of *paternalism*; to intervene against her present wishes in accordance with her past wishes is paternalistic. The paternalism will be justified if she is presently incompetent to repudiate her past wishes.[22]

Responsibility

The covenant model of therapeutic relationships provides a different context for thinking about past and present consent. The key concept here is *responsibility*—responsibility to one's covenant partners (centrally, to the patient in the case of the therapeutic covenant), and responsibility to *God* for one's dealings with one's covenant partners, since God is the pattern, witness and guardian of covenant relationships between human beings. So acting on the basis of a patient's past wish or consent is a matter of keeping a promise to the patient, living up to a commitment that one has made.

A doctor is justified in acting in accordance with his patient's present wishes, against a wish that she previously expressed, if he has been released from his previous commitment to her, or has made a new promise to her which overrides his previous promise. His decision between her present and past wishes must be made on the basis of her past and present capacity to consent. If her past wishes were expressed when she had the capacity to do so and she is judged presently

---

20 May, 'Teacher' in *The Physician's Covenant* pp 145–168; also reproduced in Lammers and Verhey (eds), *On Moral Medicine*, pp 546–555.
21 Childress, *Who Should Decide?* pp 87 ff.
22 Note, however, that Childress does not believe past consent is a sufficient condition for judging that present paternalism is justified.

incapacitated to give or refuse consent to treatment, then the doctor is bound by his past promise to her. Clearly, if she was incapacitated at the time when her previous wishes were expressed, those wishes are not binding on the doctor. But if both past and present wishes were expressed when the patient had the capacity to make such decisions, then her present consent or refusal must override her past decision.[23]

Future Consent

It is also common to appeal to *future* consent in making a present intervention in another person's life: 'You'll thank me for this when you're older!' says an exasperated parent to the child who only brushes his teeth under protest. Doctors and relatives who make decisions about an incapacitated patient's treatment may cherish the hope that, if and when the patient achieves the capacity for decision-making, he will ratify the decisions that were made on his behalf. This can seem particularly important to doctors, relatives and others when those decisions over-rule the patient's present expressed wishes, as for example in the case of a compulsory admission to psychiatric in-patient care.

Again, *responsibility* is the key to these decisions. Those who make decisions on behalf of a presently incapacitated patient exercise responsibility to the patient, and to God *for* the patient, to act as far as possible in his best interests—to do whatever is in their power to promote his well-being. They may be called to account in the future for the decisions they make. Mistakes which they make in good faith are not culpable, since certainty about a person's future best interests is frequently impossible. But if they neglect the patient's future interests or use his interests as a cloak for their own, they could be judged to have acted unethically.

Consent by Proxy

In previous sections, I have referred to 'incapacitated' patients, that is, patients who lack the capacity to make informed decisions for themselves. For such patients, decisions about their health care must be made by proxy. For example, parents may have to make such decisions on behalf of their children. However, there are narrow limits to the scope of proxy consent. I remarked in chapter four that the patient's status as human being and covenant partner is undermined if things are done to her without her consent. We can make an exception to this principle when she is incapable of giving consent to treatment which is necessary for her health or well-being; choosing treatment of this kind for her does not deny but *affirms* her worth. However, to do things to her which are *not* required for her own well-being is to place her in an unnecessarily undignified position. And to do things to her which are only in the interests of others is to treat her merely as a means to others' ends—a sheer denial of her worth as covenant partner. This restriction has obvious implications for clinical research, which I shall spell out in chapter six.

---

23 *Contra* D Parfit, *Reasons and Persons* (Oxford: Clarendon, 1984) pp 326-329.

5
Children, Covenants and Consent

I have already said that a covenant relationship requires the parties to affirm the worth of their covenant partners, and to show special concern for the interests of the weak and vulnerable. In the last section, I alluded to the special problems of cases where the patient currently lacks the capacity to give or refuse informed consent. Children are one such group of patients and are peculiarly vulnerable, as I shall outline below. I shall therefore discuss some of the special features of a therapeutic covenant in which the patient is a child.

Vulnerability

Children within therapeutic covenant relationships are vulnerable in a number of respects. Firstly, they lack much of the power which most adults have over their own lives—they are dependent on adults (especially their parents or guardians) in many ways. Secondly, they may lack the capacity that most adults have to understand their condition, and may therefore be more easily frightened by illness, injury or pain. Thirdly, they may be more easily disturbed than adults by strange or unfamiliar surroundings, such as those of a hospital. This is especially the case for very young children. The fear and disturbance caused by admission to hospital or other clinical surroundings may therefore compound the frightening effects of illness. Finally, they may lack the level of comprehension and maturity which is necessary to make informed decisions about their future and their medical care. This may mean that such decisions have to be made by proxy—by another member of the therapeutic covenant community acting on the child's behalf. Although it may be necessary, there is a danger that this in itself will compound the child's sense of not being in control, and add to her fear and vulnerability.

Proxy Consent

Who should have the responsibility of giving proxy consent on a child's behalf within a therapeutic covenant? Ideally, it should be the child's parents, because they are the ones most closely bound to the child in another, overlapping, covenant community—the family. Within the latter covenant, it is often part of the parents' role to make decisions on the child's behalf and in her best interests.

There are, of course, many cases in which parents are dead, absent or incapable of taking responsible decisions on behalf of their children. In such cases, the child needs someone to act *in loco parentis*—to assume the responsibilities that should normally fall to parents within the covenant of the family. However, the question of who should assume these responsibilities is a matter of moral and legal casuistry which is outside the scope of this booklet.

Rules

What is required of a child's therapeutic covenant partners? In particular, what is required of the parents or guardians, who bear the responsibility of proxy consent? I suggest three rules which encapsulate some of the chief requirements.

(i) Do all that you can to *minimize* the child's vulnerability

This means, for example, that the child must be informed, taught and enabled to understand as fully as possible what is happening to him—the causes of his pain or illness and what can be done to 'make him better.' Much of this role may devolve onto his parents or guardians, who are likely to be the adults he trusts most. However, they can hardly teach and inform him adequately if they themselves are kept in the dark, intentionally or unintentionally, by the doctors and other professionals who are their covenant partners. I have already noted that in the therapeutic covenant, the doctor is required to teach her patients. This is of particular importance when the patient is a child, since children are particularly vulnerable to the experience of not knowing, and lacking control over, what is happening to them.

Involvement

Furthermore, the child must be *involved* as far as possible in decisions about his care and treatment. This is, of course, heavily dependent on the age, maturity, mental health and understanding of the child. Very young children are unlikely to be able to participate to any meaningful extent in decisions affecting their future life and health. For them, information, reassurance and, above all, the caring presence of their parents are the decisive factors in minimizing their vulnerability. But if older children and teenagers are denied any involvement in decision-making, this may be very damaging and demeaning. It will reinforce the frightening impression that things are happening to them over which they have no control, and it will reduce them from covenant partners to passive participants in the therapeutic relationship.

Conflicts

The question then arises: what should be done if a young person disagrees with her parents' decisions about her treatment? For example, may she refuse treatment to which her parents have given proxy consent? Legally, the situation is complex. In England and Wales, children with sufficient understanding and intelligence can consent to treatment, regardless of age.[24] However, there is case law which suggests that they may not *refuse* treatment if proxy consent has been given by someone *in loco parentis*.[25] Be that as it may, my covenantal account of consent implies that if a child or young person can be shown to have sufficient

---

24 *The Ethical Conduct of Research on Children* (London: Medical Research Council, 1991) pp 15-16.
25 D Dickenson, 'Children's informed consent to treatment: is the law an ass?' *J Med Ethics*, vol 20 (1994) pp 205-206, 222.

maturity, understanding and mental health to make important decisions about her own life, she should be free to give *or refuse* consent to treatment. There may be situations in which parents ought to respect a young person's refusal of treatment, even though the law gives them the power to overrule it.

(ii) Do nothing to *exploit* the child's vulnerability

Because the child in a therapeutic covenant is to a large extent in the power of others, these others must be especially careful not to exploit or abuse that power. In particular, this means that there must be limits to the scope of proxy consent. As I argued at the end of the last chapter, proxy consent may only be given for procedures that are intended to benefit the child directly.

(iii) Act, to the best of your knowledge and ability, so as to promote the child's *shalom*

This rule does not need very much explanation but two points are worth drawing out. Firstly, *shalom* means very much more than just physical well-being, even in a medical context. Emotional and spiritual well-being and other factors play a part as well. Indeed, there are cases where there is no realistic hope of curing a terminal illness, and the child's well-being is best served by abandoning therapies which may merely cause unnecessary pain and prolong the process of dying. However, these are extreme cases. Such decisions should not be made lightly by adult patients on their own behalf; they are very grave decisions indeed when made by proxy on behalf of a child.

Secondly, it is worth noting the difficulty for parents and guardians of being honest and clear-sighted about the child's interests, particularly in tragic and distressing cases. In situations such as the one I have just envisaged, where treatment can do no further good, some parents may nonetheless be tempted to demand continued (ultimately futile) efforts to cure the child. Conversely, some parents may refuse life-saving treatment in cases where the child *could* benefit. For example, it has sometimes been the practice to withhold relatively simple and life-saving surgery from babies with Down's syndrome, claiming that this was in the patient's best interests.[26] But to justify this practice one must show that most people with Down's syndrome have such a poor quality of life that they would have been better off dying in infancy—a claim that is very hard to sustain. In such cases, the parents' judgment about the child's best interests may be clouded by their own inability or unwillingness to cope with the child's condition.

Given these difficulties, it is very important that doctors and other professionals in the therapeutic covenant play a part in helping the parents to discern the child's best interests. This is partly connected with the doctor's role as teacher, helping the parents to understand the child's condition and prognosis. However, it also involves supporting the parents so that they can find the courage and

---

26 *Euthanasia and Clinical Practice: Trends, Principles and Alternatives* (London: Linacre Centre, 1982) pp 5-6.

strength to act genuinely in the child's interests. The doctor may need to call on others, such as ministers or chaplains, within the therapeutic covenant in order to make this support available—but it remains in some measure his role.

6
Consent to Research

Therapeutic and Non-therapeutic
In this chapter, I shall use the term 'clinical research' to denote any research using human subjects. It will be necessary to distinguish further between *therapeutic* and *non-therapeutic* research. In therapeutic research there is the intention of direct benefit to the patient who is the research subject; one example is a clinical trial to compare the effectiveness of two different treatments for the same disease. Non-therapeutic research may mean anything from the safety-testing of a new drug on healthy volunteers to the taking of blood or urine samples for epidemiological research. Involvement in a non-therapeutic research project may *indirectly* benefit the subject and others, but there is no intention that a patient's condition will be directly improved if he acts as a subject of non-therapeutic research.

It is worth pointing out that there are good ethical reasons why non-therapeutic research should be done. Many diseases could be better treated if they were better understood, and doctors have a responsibility to their patients to ensure that the care they are offered is based on the best possible scientific evidence. That said, a covenantal understanding of medical ethics and informed consent sets limits on what may be done in clinical research, because no covenant partner may be used merely as a means to the end of benefitting others.

1. Research Involving Adults

A subject's involvement in a clinical research project must be seen within the context of a therapeutic covenant relationship. In many cases, the clinical investigator is also the subject's doctor. But even if she is not, she enters into a relationship with him which is very closely related to the doctor-patient covenant. She accepts a responsibility to care for his well-being, and to see that it is not unnecessarily compromised by the research project. If she is not the subject's own general practitioner, she will need to maintain good communication with the GP in order to ensure that the subject's well-being is adequately cared for.

Consent to Research
One particular responsibility of the clinical investigator is to ensure that the subject's consent to research is free and informed. I have referred in chapter four

to the danger of concealed coercion in therapeutic relationships. This danger is particularly acute in clinical research. Anyone who has worked in scientific or medical research knows that there can be great pressure on the researcher to complete a project successfully. Feeling such pressures, she may be tempted to exert undue influence in persuading potential subjects to participate. Because of this, it is more important than ever that clinical investigators are scrupulous in respecting subjects' freedom to refuse to participate in a research project, or to withdraw at any time.

Guidelines
In the light of these comments, I suggest a few guidelines which should be observed by clinical investigators using adult research subjects, although this is by no means an exhaustive list.

(i) Therapeutic Research
1. If the experimental therapy which is to be tried is particularly risky or untested, it should *only* be offered to patients for whom no established therapy is available, or for whom there is no reasonable prospect of any established therapy working. For example, when transplant surgery was being developed in the 1960s and 1970s, early recipients of transplanted organs had poor life expectancies. It would clearly have been unethical to offer experimental transplants to patients for whom other forms of treatment held out the prospect of many years of life.
2. More generally, all reasonable steps should be taken to ensure that the clinical outcome for a patient is not made significantly worse by her participation in the research project. For example, in trials of new drugs, it is often appropriate to provide patients with a 'rescue medication' which they can use if the experimental drug regime fails to relieve their symptoms. There is almost always some risk involved in clinical research, as there is in almost any medical treatment. But in clinical research, everything possible must be done to ensure that the risk is minimized.

(ii) Non-therapeutic Research
1. Clearly, the principle that the risk should be minimized also applies to non-therapeutic research—particularly since, by definition, there is no significant prospect of clinical benefit to the subject to balance against the risk.
2. In addition, particular care should be given to the recruitment of subjects for non-therapeutic research. Hans Jonas has suggested a procedure for minimizing the danger of concealed coercion:[27] the first to be recruited should be those who have the greatest understanding of the research, the greatest identification with its aims and the greatest freedom from external pressure to partici-

---

27 H Jonas, 'Philosophical Reflections on Experimenting with Human Subjects,' in Lammers and Verhey (eds), *On Moral Medicine*, pp 616-627.

pate. Jonas' criteria suggest that the first to be recruited should be members of the research community, then other members of the general population, and 'least and last of all the sick.' Likewise, Paul Ramsey advises caution in enrolling prisoners as research subjects, since they are likely to be less free than others from external pressures.[28]

2. Research Involving Children

Much of what I have already written, particularly about therapeutic research, also applies to children. However, additional constraints apply to children who lack the capacity to give informed consent to research. I argued in previous chapters that proxy consent may only be given when the patient's own well-being requires it and that to break this rule is an unnecessary exercise of power over a vulnerable individual. Therefore I conclude that proxy consent may only be given to *therapeutic* research, and then only if the following conditions are met: (1) that there is no established therapy which is likely to be more effective than the experimental therapy; (2) that the risks of the experimental therapy are proportionate to the seriousness of the child's condition or the hoped-for benefit to the child. Proxy consent may not be given to *non-therapeutic* research, even if there is minimal risk of harm.[29]

However, many legal minors might show themselves, by virtue of maturity, understanding and other criteria, to be capable of giving free and informed consent. If so, they may be recruited as subjects of non-therapeutic research, but only under the most stringent regulation. Regulatory authorities should not approve any non-therapeutic research project involving consenting minors if the same results could be gained without involving minors. They should also be most reluctant to approve any such research project carrying more than minimal risk.[30]

Because there is no intention of direct benefit to the patient, extra caution needs to be exercised in seeking minors' consent to non-therapeutic research. The danger of concealed coercion is also especially acute since many young people are particularly vulnerable to pressure from adults. For these reasons, the agreement of the parents or guardians should normally be obtained, though for young people living independently this may not be appropriate. As an additional safeguard against concealed coercion, young people's capacity to consent to non-therapeutic research should be assessed, and their consent sought, by appropriately trained professionals who are *not involved* in the research project. There is a great deal to be said for involving ministers (such as hospital or health care chaplains) in such consent procedures.

28 Ramsey, *The Patient as Person*, pp 41-44.
29 This is the position taken by Paul Ramsey in *The Patient as Person*, pp 11ff; it conflicts with guidelines published by the Medical Research Council (*op cit*, note 25) and others, which do allow minimal-risk non-therapeutic research involving children.
30 See *Guidelines for the Ethical Conduct of Medical Research Involving Children* (London: British Paediatric Association, 1992) p 9 for the distinction between minimal, low and high risk. For example, taking a urine sample would be considered a minimal-risk procedure, but taking a blood sample a low-risk procedure.

7
Conclusions

In this booklet, I have given one Christian account of doctor-patient relationships and informed consent, grounded in the theology of covenant love. Much of the practical outworking may not be new to many doctors. One possible reason for this is that if we are created in the image of a covenanting God, then at our best we will tend to behave covenantally. Another is that Western medicine has fairly deep roots in religious (including Christian) traditions, without always being aware of the fact. It is helpful to articulate these traditions, since they spell out the reasons for adopting certain standards of good medical practice.

My account, however, may also challenge some aspects of medical practice and put a question-mark against some systems of health care provision. In Chapter One I observed that the practice of health care professionals does not always measure up to covenant standards. I also remarked that any health care *system* which inhibits the flourishing of covenant relationships must be found wanting by the standards of Christian medical ethics.

Christians who are involved in the health and caring professions may have a specially important role to play in promoting covenant relationships in medicine. For example, they may be called to be living examples of covenant standards in their professional lives, insofar as it is in their power to do so. They may also have the opportunity to be advocates for a covenantal framework, arguing that it is a more adequate foundation for therapeutic relationships than some of its rivals. And sometimes they may be called to play a prophetic role in challenging the system or its practitioners when practice falls short of the standards set by the covenant.

Droving

by
Matt Mooney

Published 2003 by Matt Mooney.

Copyright Matt Mooney.

All Rights Reserved. No part of this publication may be reproduced, stored in a retrieval system, or transmitted in any form, or by any means, electronic, mechanical, photocopying, recording or otherwise, witout the permission of the publisher. He asserts his right under the Copyright, Designs and Patent Act, 1988 to be identified as the author of this work.

Cover photograph and design by Méabh Mooney.

Printing and overall design Walsh Colour Print.

ISBN

RÉAMHRÁ

Glacaim go fonnmhar le cuireadh an údair cúpla focal a chur le chéile mar réamhrá chun an leabhar filíochta seo a sheoladh ar mhuir mhór na litríochta.

I deem it a great privilege to respond to my friend and fellow thespian's request to pen a few lines, by way of introduction, to his collection of poetry and verses. Trilingually (Irish, English and French) the poems like the Red Admiral butterfly, emerge from the chrysalis that is Matt's fertile mind, to encapsulate and capture forever a kaleidescope of seasons, landscapes, personalities, emotions, situations and images that soar skyward to the stars. Through his love of nature, his fellow man (and woman) allied to an astute observation of the epiphanies of the day , he skillfully takes, transforms, burnishes and versifies the mundane, to be read and enjoyed by us lesser mortals, with a novel and enlightening perspective. A couplet from his poem "Voyage" struck a particular chord with me:

"Look! - a light on peaceful shore
Where voyagers' thoughts can all outpour."

I invite the reader to share and enjoy the felicity of the experience of Matt's thoughts and outpourings and sail away on a transport of pure delight.

Traoslaím leis ar a shaothar. Guím rath Dé ar féin agus a chlann agus, i dtaobh an chnuasacht seo, mar a deir an seanfhocal-
"Go néirí leis go maith is go geal fé mar a dúirt an fear nuair a chuir sé a léine sa dath!"

Garry McMahon

Short Biography

Matt was born in Woodville, Cill Chríost near Loughrea in 1943.
Youngest of eight children growing up on the family farm.
Vocational teacher in Listowel since 1966.
Married to Mary with three daughters: Anne, Méabh and Siobhán.

Contents

Wild Roses	1
Serenade to Silence	3
Forgotten Author	4
Instant Everything	5
Aromas	5
The Instrument	6
An Vic	7
The Vic	8
Rún	9
A Secret	9
Firewatch	10
From Aghadoe	10
Anniversaire	11
Birthday	11
Cruach Mhárthain	12
Méabh	13
Children	13
Bog Beauty	14
Brandon	15
Thirst	15
The Hunter Boy	16
Looking Up	17
From Salthill	18
The Light	19
Pendulum	19
An Ghaillimh	20
Galway	20
Máirtín-m'Athair	21
Máirtín my Father	22
Voyage	23
Droving	24
Final Swim	25
Bryan	26
La Paloma	27
Her First Confession	28
The Teacher	28
Loch Riach	29
Near Cuckoo Lane	30
Minor to Major	30
Pool of Dreams	31

Tartan	32
Drums	32
Pastel Beauty	33
Whiff	33
The Shearing	34
Chic	34
Chariot Wheels	35
Eye to Eye	35
Raidió Dé	36
Radio God	36
Solas Draíochta	37
Magic Light	38
Penalty Points	39
Deadlines	40
L'Aube d'Avril	41
The April Dawn	42
Ode to a Sausage	43
West Clare	44
Black Gloves	45
Tarbert	46
On Waves of Love	47
Exiled in Aldershot	48
Star Flight	49
Gap in the Wind	50
The Driver	51
Pierced	51
The Strength of Love	52
Lá Márta	53
March Day	54
Ears of Oats	54
High Tide	55
A Wandering Spirit	56
Cailín an Lomaire Faiche	57
The Lawn-mower Lady	57
The Worker Bee	58
Concerto	58
Autumn Gifts	59
In Step	60
Humpty Dumpty Eile	61
Another Humpty Dumpty	62
Pearl	62
Hawthorns	63
Little Hands	63

Wild Roses

Still I see these wild red roses
Right beside the meadow gate,
With your face framed by the dying sun,
Your long black hair in place -
The perfect setting for your warm love
In your softly smiling face.

Summer strolls to milk the bog-field cows
By cow-slipped meadow paths,
To later strain and skim and store
The cream in earthen jars
By chimney side for churning
When the hay was made and tied.

So steadfast in the quest for happiness
For the family growing strong,
While Martin ploughed from headlands
Where the tea they gladly drank;
The sea gulls in a hail of white
Flew low and swooped and dived
In a tribute to the couple
By the furrows of their lives.

From fields to growing family cares
She tended both the same;
In stringent times she added love
When nought else was at hand,
Making savings so our futures could be bright.

She lived and prayed through this century
And so, she died in ninety-nine;
From the girl by the mountain stream
Where the ducklings wild swam free,
To the joys of her great-grandchildren -
Still the lady of her dreams.

Strong and steadfast loving mother,
Never losing youthful cheer,
Here's a toast to one so lovely
Climbing heaven's golden stairs.

Serenade to Silence

Two crows noiselessly crawl
Black winged in the blue coolness,
Trying not to waken
The silent sleeping fields
Of October grass soft and lush,
The late lover sun embracing
The passionate green land.

Down the windless tunnel,
The hawthorned red hawed bóithrín,
I walk in peace,
Blackberries scenting sweetly;
Cregg Castle on the stony hill
Looking west across the silver turlough,
Where our cattle drank all summer.

With snowflake softness,
And moonlight tenderness
The robin sings two notes,
While the grasshopper too
Clicks his own conclusion
To the silent serenade.

"Forgotten Author"

On a soft Sunday duskness,
Our hate torn island yields
A match of football prowess
On the altar of Croke Park's peace.

Some long dead romantic's music
Awakens the strong strings of life,
Buried deep in our chests,
Dissolving political battering.

Some small offering, unknown,
Turns back the hands of time,
An accidental drop soothing
Like sweet rain after thirst.

All the good is hidden,
Unheeded by the mass
Of wounded souls sorrowing,
Closing fists in hatred.

The system sways and shakes,
Children cry quietly, inwardly,
Soldiers are no Santa Clauses.
Saracens pause, roll and roar.

The science of life confounded,
The outspreading life tree
Sheds its dead leaves
On the Emerald Isle.

Instant Everything

The thronging thousands search for a way
To end the waiting, even at a dance.
So many know the song is old yet new;
Forever, right or wrong it happened before.

By gesture or expression no sword hangs poised.
Whose soul will speak tonight to a kindred spirit?
No price to pay inside these purgatorial walls,
No hell here, just emptiness - love search endless.

So many fifty pieces of silver passed and paid
Through small windows to faceless marketeers,
Unconscious of their role as he who sold his God
For thirty pieces, walking the other way as well.

In the stranglehold of society set on self destruction,
Materialisticly mothered I struggle, shrugging off
The consequences of exploitation; on this hard road,
Showband signed, I lose my identity for now.

Aromas

Because I learned my lessons by lamplight,
The scent of parrafin sealing family love
Forever in my senses,
You too can learn in love
From books and incense;
Candles so coloured on your windowsill
Against the black of night.

The Instrument

Joe Burke's accordion,
Yet lying in it's box beside us
Electrifies our senses in waiting!
When thrown open
By the mighty master
And stretched to it's first few notes
Before the frenzy,
Its cover of travel stained wood is forgotten.
Like the birth of a butterfly,
Music glides free
From the caterpillar of one day into another,
Until from below proud eyes
And beard of silver sheen,
Looking into the pool of our lives,
He grows legs, tails and heads
To frogs who leap about
Within their lives circle,
Jumping clear into clean air
To live a new life -
Born for the interpretation of the dance
That dormant lies basely in our brain.
All becoming one mind to music,
Drawing it in fresh
Till it touches it's home
In the heart of whoever we are -
Till he himself becomes the instrument in the session.

An Vic

Chuimlíos an vic led'dhroim
Ar a dó sa dorchadas.
Bhain do throm chasachtaigh
Cloigín i mo cheann
Ag scaipeadh brionglóidí
A luíonn liom go fánach.
Léimeas óm'luí san oíche,
Clocha sneachta go tréan
Ar phána na fuinneoige,
Is codhladh mo pháistín briste.

Chuimlíos an vic ar d'ucht
Is bhraitheas na cnámha boga
A mhúnlaíomar-mise is do mham,
Iad so-bhriste daonúil diaga
Mar phalás dod'chroí.
A leanbhín na h-oíche,
Féileachán girsiúil misniúil,
Chodail tú arís gan bhac
Is chuas ar thóir an tobac,
Mar ghadaí i ngáirdín Dé.

The Vick

Your cough in the night
Was calling for a cure
So I rubbed the Vick
On your baby back.
As the dreams of the night
Evaporated,
Hailstones on the window pane
Stole your sleep as well.

Your troubled chest a cage so soft,
The palace of your heart,
Such a fragile and divine creation
Conceived.
Child of ours and of the night,
Brave butterfly of a girl,
You slipped away to sleep
As I tiptoed for tobacco
Like a thief in God's garden.

Rún

Níl aon ní níos áille dom
Ná mo leanbh ag lorg cíche
Ag diúl di féin
San réim rúndiamhar
Nach eol d'éinne beo
Ach í féin amháin;
Nach buairt di anois
Ach bainne bán na beatha.

A Secret

Nothing was ever so beautiful
As from the secret place you drank
The pure white milk of life
Your one and only source of joy.

Firewatch

Turf and timber feed the fire.
Sitting, talking to a child,
Barring out the November night,
Bathing in the pool of end-day,
Surfaced on the calm finteán.
Flames to burn out the pain
To fill the mind with peace -
Reflections of ourselves.

From Aghadoe

You left me with the loneliness of bare hills
Against the evening sky, where sunset shades
Of brown and black splashed wildly
Forever now will dance with me.

I raked the floors of hell with spurs of eager love,
Fallen far with secrets sore locked up from far above;
I planned by night and day to set us free from nought,
Your answer was to me a "maybe" and so I sought.

Cold glow of each day born, nights their memories hold,
Never you'll come to me till secret love is sold;
Holding hands of hope on palms of sorrow,
With friends so long ago, we'd sung of a new tomorrow.

Anniversaire

Après minuit,
Entre la Toussaint
Et la fête des morts
Anne naquit -
Ma fille,
Seize ans.
Après -
Étoile de ma vie
Depuis son enfance
Jusqu'à cette nuit.

Birthday

After midnight,
Between All Saints
And All Souls,
Anne was born -
My daughter
Of sixteen.

Afterwards -
Light of my life
From her birth
To this night.

Cruach Mhárthain

One by one the shadows pass
Across the face of Márthan,
The blue eyed brown haired lovely lass
Finds mountain climbing warm.

We climbed and scrambled to the peak
And many times we rested,
At times we sat and felt so weak
We thought it had us bested.

Up and up and then we sank
Like snowflakes on the ground,
We felt so free as deep we drank
The beauty all around.

From Carraig Hill we ruled the world,
A man was cutting hay beneath,
On a regal rock in comfort curled,
We shivered as the breeze blew oe'r the heath.

Méabh

As the sun is setting on Kerry Head,
A backdrop for a great dark cloud
Gliding to the south ominously -
The little girl slips quietly in
To sink in sleep in the cosy room,
The light of sky falling softly
Around the sleeping happy child.
The turf fire comes to life
In rays of warm gold.
Soon the sounds so faint subside
As her breathing turns to dreaming.

Children

See the romping children
Send their joy to heaven,
Listen to their voices
Talking to your mind
In your sun sapping body;
Sanded and splashed
By flying feet
You come alive
Beside this sea,
This edge of earthlings,
These symbols of our destiny.

Bog Beauty

We'd wander both
In this wild place
Where the Pilibín,
Excited in her role
Of mother to grey chicks,
Somewhere on a turtóg
In the sacred riasc,
Scarce blends her call
With the mionnán aerach.

We'd walk hand in hand
By the yellow flaggers
Flowering in the river bed.
We'd sit on wooden posts
Resting oe'r the stream
And dance our toes
In the smooth balm of bogs.

Slaked with thirst
We'd fall on the well's edge
And dip our faces down
To drink from our mother earth,
United side by side.
As evening vibrates
With mionnán aerach exultance
I feel the Pilibíns are impatient,
Seeking their own peace,
Calling me parasite in their paradise.

We'd stay and weave a coverlet
From the ceannabháin.
The crows would surely call us
In the bog brisk dawn
As they swoop from trees above
In the tall woods beside us.

Brandon

My spirit rests on mountains west
Alone up there with truth,
Among the maze of mountain paths
Rough rocks and ravines ravaged,
Where snow untouched untarnished rests -
Pure white transient proof
That God alone up there
Silently holds something for Himself
Beyond the grasp of man,
But not the gaze of poets.

Thirst

Down below the Champs-Éleysées,
In Charles de Gaulle Étoile
I saw her drinking deeply
As she stood on platform one.
She was tall and black and beautiful
In the August afternoon,
An ebony woman waiting -
The soul of the African sun.

The Hunter Boy

I know a man, a grey haired man,
Whose dreams took shape,
While yet a hunter boy -
A dozen years or so he said,
Fleet as youth,
He nearly grasped the unknown of time.

On the demesne wall it stood,
Too bold to be a fairy.
Away, away he leaps to grasp,
The illusive, bright and airy elf,
Nostrils quivering, legs flying,
Seconds intervening alluringly.

The hare and hound
No faster ran
Than man and Mammon flew.
The elf his treasure held,
A purse of sovereign gold,
A gréasaí leipreachán we're told!

Faster ran the dream of dreams,
From demesne wall,
Bare feet screaming o'er the grass,
Boy spiralling hands to catch -
Ready for a clinch;
Would his world cascade confetti?

No cascade came,
But grassy, earthy arms
Compassed this elf before his eyes.
It was no ordinary ground,
But a lios or fort for elfin folk,
Of elfin folk, magically mystifying.

We are each The Hunter Boy,
We know not what we follow,
A slant of sunshine,
A river flowing seaward,
Waltzed by the breath of life
Towards our dreamy sea.

Looking Up

Rising o'er old Aughty's rim
The sun spawns golden light,
Leaping o'er the frosted fields
Where cattle crib-like stand.
High above the tractor tracks
The whirring wings surprise -
Two swans with merry sounds
Wheel south o'er the lonely land.

From Salthill

Between the mountains merrily
The Gaeltacht people dance together,
Celtic carnival of voice and violin.
The old men gain silence,
Singing songs of all ages
Of love or war or loss.
Young men feeling brotherhood,
Waiting on the words of Gaelic.

Over on the Aran Islands
Black against the evening's veil
Of red muslin, silver streaked,
The old stock of our land -
Hard and weathered old men
Are restless in a listless nation.

Buy them there a drink
For though they're singing now
They may silence all too soon
Like the startled singing bird.
These are the unconquered
Free voices of Ireland,
Proud of their ancestry.

Purple now the hills of Clare;
The sun stands on Silver Strand,
Blinding in it's brilliance.
On the tourist trodden promenade
Girls silhouetted stroll together.

The Light

Along the grove's soft floor
A pine crawled for life,
Reaching for the sun
With antennaed end
At the first sign of light
Between it's brother trees
Keeping it in the dark.
Small sand dune oak
By the sea in Jard Sur Mer,
Fat and bare of bark,
Dead reptile - still with dignity.

Pendulum

Time holds stern hand
Dimming sips of life,
Dull heavy clangs
Driving here and back.

Walled limits of sixty seven,
Smash it! deny it!
Let the hands swing free
And take some other prisoner.

We are the fools of time
Yet, men are born free -
Never to die.
Time is man's servant!

An Ghaillimh

Meán lae saoire mí Iúil na gréine
Lámh le Moons na mbrat is na mbláth,
Ollstór an chúinne i gcathair na dtreabh.
Cos mhuintir na cruinne ar Shráid an tSiopa,
Is mé ag faire ar phéire dealbh
Péinteálta ina dtost
Ag tarraingt an tslua.

Maor tráchta ag scríobh ticeád páirceála,
Is Tomás an tSean-nóis ard is aerach
Mac Eoin na n-amhrán ag gabháil thart.
Boscadóir sráide ina shuí cois falla,
Méara ag brú is ag crú an cheoil -
Fear dall stuama mar iascaire bradán
Ar bhruach na habhann ag faire srutha.

Galway

Holiday mid day in sunny July
By Moon's of flags and flowers,
Corner store, city of the tribes.
In crowded Shop Street
I watch a pair of statues
Painted into silence
Drawing us ever closer.

A traffic warden writing tickets,
As tall Tomás of the Sean-Nós
Mac Eoin of the songs goes by.
Street busker by the wall
Milking music from the box,
Blind and patient fisherman
By the river of humanity.

Máirtín - m'Athair

Dallóga leath-druidte idir é
Agus an pháirc ghlas ghrianmhar,
É leath bhealaigh síos bóithrín na marbh,
Caoraigh ag iníor ar thaobh an chnoic,
Iad aclaí ach ramhar agus olannach go talamh.
Tuige fuinneoga ag am mar seo?
De ghnáth feictear im-shaol laethúil tíortha,
Ach sa chás seo is féachaint siar é -
A shaol ag sleamhnú síos fáinne an chnoic.
Cé acu is tábhachtaí anois - gaol nó gaire?

Gloine idir spideog agus a saol dúchais,
Idir leanbh agus iontasaí atá le teacht.
Gloine mar phána, mar bhac do-thuigthe, so-fheichte,
Ach i gcás duine breoite scáthán cuimhní fánacha;
Paiste glas ag síor laghdú is an t-eitleán ag ardú,
Á cheangailt fós le cumhacht na bpréamh,
Le snaidhm an ghrá; a óige, a shláinte gan omos.
Uilecheangail na sclábhaíochta in iarthar na hÉireann
Ar maidin is um iarnóin, slí bheatha á ríomh
Dó féin is dá chlann mhac is iníon taobh leis,
A lámha spréite le teann díchill -
Clocha crithir criadh á gcaitheamh go leath-taobh
Ó ríocht na beatha is síor-thocailte.

Nó é i móinéar mín i mí na n-uan
Le dul faoi na gréine um Cháisc.
Féar tirim a lúiodh roimhe is é ar a inneall bainte
Lá samhraidh, ina sraitheanna umhla cumhra;
Maraon leis an saol is amhrán ina bhéal -
An feirmeoir croíúil cumhachtach aerach
Ar a bhealach ó cheann 'ceann na páirce,
Fuiseoga os a chionn á mholadh is ag adhradh na gréine,
Ceol Dé gan fhios dóibh.

Máirtín my Father

Half drawn blinds on a sunny green field,
He was halfway down the road to death.
Sheep grazing on the hillside,
Fat but lively balls of wool;
What good are windows to him now?
Looking back and looking out at life
Slipping away from him before his eyes,
Till people matter more than place.

Glass between a robin and it's freedom,
Between a child and wonders yet to come;
Invisible pane of mystery barring -
But to the sick- mirrors of memories.
Green field steadily fading,
His flight is ready to go, yet tied
To love, lost health and all life's labours.
Western man with his family farming,
His hands were splayed from working,
Taking stones from soil aside
In the tillage fields of Woodville.

Or in his finest field at sunset
When Easter lambs were everywhere.
On a Summer's day the hay would fall beside him,
Mowed in humble swathes so sweet;
One with the world he'd sing his songs,
The strong and hearty farmer.

Headland to headland he'd mow
And the larks poured out their praise.
For God and man they sang,
They loved the sun and all that God created.

Voyage

The rushing, stopping currents cold,
A thousand straining thoughts not told.
The wheels of plotting, planning aim -
A puzzle pieced, still life's a plain.

Swinging high on heights escaled
Changing course when we had failed,
New laurels crowning patient brows,
Has time stood still - no end allows?

Will the powers on high reshape the spirit
Pour in life's liquid fire to fill it?
Look! - a light on peaceful shore
Where voyagers' thoughts can all outpour!

Droving

My flock of padding sheep I'm droving
Driving down the bóithrín way,
Having drunken dip-day memories,
High on heat and crazing smells.
Seen the sheep at their immersion
For their annual cleansing swim,
Emerging wet and so insulted
At being thrown into the deep!
By the field of rock and fern
By the Deerpark ambling by,
While the starlings all in harmony
Keep us company for a while.
Blackened chimney crocks on houses
Where my Galway neighbours live
Are a contrast to the castle -
Roxboro's memory to the French,
Norman ruins-roofless smokeless,
And later past the red Grand Gate;
In that avenue lived Lady Gregory
In the days of the poet Yeats.
Outside the Cottage Grove is sitting
A cheeky rabbit achewing the cud,
While at the cross of Isserkelly
A total stranger for us stood.

Final Swim

Sky never so blue
In the last gasps
Of the day.
Low tide revealing
Sands so smooth,
Black rock balcony
On the tall cliff
Thrills romantics -
Like Siobhán the swimmer!
"Romeo and Juliet" she says,
Looking up, dripping wet,
Walking from a dream
On the waves outside,
Her fair hair glistening.
Daly's windows
A golden fire
Across the beach;
Sun dips seawards
Towards America,
Above the small birds fly.
The final strollers stare
At two silent silver jets
Flying East
In the darkening dome.

Bryan

Marked absent!
What's that he's left behind?
There's love and pride
From the village chief,
Kerry gold down every street
Where people stop to talk,
To look and say it's this
Or that, and lean against the wall,
To watch it all and wish it well -
The stream of life going by.
Yes, the footpaths of the living
Are for talking too you see -
Though it's simple things you say,
They sometimes make
Such awful sense for you're
Present here today.

La Paloma

Bunny Dalton's dead,
Endgame to Listowel
That's lost him.
Light-fingered on the accordion
Often outside his door
Caressing the day in summer
With 'La Paloma'
Down his street
Of low built houses of stone-
As dignified as himself
Merriment masqued,
Waiting with baited wit.
The sunlit Square sees
His leaving.
Stretching his arms
The Sunday paper man
Closes the till shut
On another Mass morning.
Now two men emerge
To pitch and putt today,
Striding towards the Lawn
Past St. Mary's Church
Where the clock's stopped,
Pendulum poised.

Her First Confession

Nor yet she knows as she kneels
In the silence of the church
On an April evening of prayer
Saying to the seated priest,
"This is my first confession,"
That up in Heaven
God the Father too He sits
And strains to hear her voice
Floating from the earth below -
My child of seven, sinless angel.

The Teacher

The first alarm call from our hillside thrush
Froze us into silent wonder.
The daily drama dawned at our doorstep
With the eager morning talk
Of three steps of stairs to life schoolboys,
Waiting for their lift to school -
Unaware of my wariness to face the arena
And the mind flexing thought stretching task;
But I taught that day then closed the book.
Evening was full of memories of all the fun,
The frowns or laughter on their faces young.
I drew the mantle of the night over all our cares,
And we retreated to the level plains of love.

Loch Riach

The grey lake and the bare shore,
The pleasure boat that's tied at bay,
Washed summer sun whispers amour,
Loch Riach rolls restless today.

Her shore side towns' a stranger dour,
Its Lake Road holds no girl of gaiety,
Her streets are dull, her people sour,
St. Brendan's bells regret the deity.

The tennis court it too has died,
No gay youths frolic in summer whites,
The Long Point pulls the crowd aside
Though the lake rolls restless these nights.

But the grey will change to moonlit gold
On a dais shall sit the deity,
The bells will ring and flags unfold
For Loch Riach's young queen of the laity.

Near Cuckoo Lane

At five a.m. in Killocrim
The rounded notes of Paradise
Escaped from the cuckoo's
Thieving sweet soft throat,
Transfiguring a new day
With her song of summer.

Minor to Major

Like a church, in the Bons below
There's an old model mortuary
With a slated roof and cross,
White walled, twin doored:
In and out they'd go
To bid the dead goodbye,
Out to breathe the day.
How small it all seems
Set against Sliabh Mish,
Majestic in the morning,
Mists lifting overhead
While silver doves are spiralling
Like incense o'er the town,
Against the mountain face.
Floating, flashing to and fro
Joyfully alive, the friendly flock
Ascend like smoke signals
From eternal destinations.

Pool of Dreams

Sitting down beside the glass walls of the pool
I watch our children and their friends at swim
On and under water, always full of zip.
While the stronger ones went diving dove like
The little ones were paddled by their auntie Anne.
Suddenly my three years baby girl lost her grip
Slipping underwater in this fishbowl eerie world!
All I was went diving with her as I froze!
Then her auntie Anne retrieved her wonderfully.
My heart resumed its rhythm and I sighed
Seeing how the little diver had survived!
Still I sat and all the children disappeared,
I was sitting by an empty glass walled pool;
Were there really any children in my life?
Were they mine those beings in the bubble glass?

Thank God I see them coming from the showers,
Quickly dressed uncombed and happy on their way!
I rise to follow all the children of my dreams.

Tartan

You came down the street in a tartan cloak,
Like a princess with your gold-lit hair -
Graceful as a sailing boat.
When you talked with me
I walked in the Valley of Spring.

Drums

Once from a pipe rough with red paint
Rainwater fell fresh as baby grass,
Fresh as youth nestled in a lair of love;
Vibrantly vital as the western farmer
Striding in when ropes were tied,
His hay winds standing safe.
Raindrops sounded yesteryear
On a foreign semi-attic sill -
No heart beat with my heart
But the drops were the drums of God

Pastel Beauty

The apple blossom of her cheeks and lips,
Her Spanish lace at student dance,
Oft haughty words and verbal grips
Were quick forgot in melting glance.

How well she sang one evening early
As by my side she walked awhile,
To keep her by I could but barely -
My God but 'twas a pleasant mile.

The curling pins she wore that day
Were but a crown on my love's hair;
Her presence lifted gloom away -
'Twas daffodilled as April air.

Whiff

Whiff of turf smoke
In the bog's own bank
Intoxicates me!
Remembering it
Reroots me
In my simplicity.

The Shearing

It is the night before the shearing of the sheep;
Last night I tried to drown the pain I felt
On that Corpus Christi noon -
Her fragrant hair blew wild across my face;
I grew so cold-that kind of cold
That creeps into a prisoner's soul,
Alone and unbelieving

It is the night before the shearing of the sheep;
The evening was exposed in tangent beauty,
Spreading from the hills.
The clouds are hanging in chandeliers of black
O'er the bogs and creggs and cowslipped meadows.
From the slopes of night comes an oboe bleat -
Poor lamb too tired of day,
Happy in the last streaks of grey.

Chic

Graceful lady in Grafton St,
Of slow measured step
To the swing of her hips;
Disappearing with dignity
To the click of her heels.

Chariot Wheels

The rumble of his cart by Cooks
Filled with turnips from Tanavalla,
The land he loved and had to leave;
The hand of health closing in it's palm
Strength of life loved and spent.
Horse and cart by Coolnaleen Cross
Facing for Finuge and home.
Sunburnt, strong, capless and heedless of time,
Today he died a happy man still.
Rolling on to heaven on chariot wheels,
Ready to greet his God,
As he greeted you and I -
Smiling with peace in his heart.

Eye to Eye

Blue eyes of a child
In the high house of prayer,
Our eyes casting down
From each other, each one;
Looking each eye to eye
Its Christ's face we'd see.
Look at that child
In the cathedral there,
So small and he smiled
Seeming to say-why so
Are you here for to pray?
So why are we blind
To the presence of Christ?
It's so plain to see
We need the eyes of a child.

Raidió Oé

Guth ar an aer iar- Nollaig,

Craoltóir croíúil caoin
A d'aithris dán dúinn -
"Lead kindly Light,"
Ó Thrá-lí do ghuí go ciúin -
Cumha is ceol le chéile.

Do dhoras druidte
Ach cloisimid.

Radio God

Voice on the after Christmas air,
Warm and kind hearted lady
With the words of 'Lead kindly Light';
Soft music, maybe melancholy,
Your prayer from Tralee
Comes through closed doors.

Solas Draoíchta

Ná h-imigh ó'm thaobhsa anocht
A chailín seang donn
Is ní chaillfear greim docht
Ar snáth síoda an Luan.

Cím milseacht na meala
Id' shúilibh séimh diamhar
Castar brat led'fholt álainn
Ar mo smaoínte atá grámhar.

Is cruaidh craptha mo chroí
Le pianta buan géar,
Is uaigneach mo luí
Im'leaba im'dhaor.

Ná coinnigh an coinneal
Id'lámh gan a lasadh,
Scaip gruaim na cruinne
Atá an-mhall ag casadh.

Magic Light

Don't leave my side tonight
My slender auburn girl,
We might break the thread of silk
That binds us both since Monday.

There's the sweetness of honey
In your soft divine eyes
And your hair so alluring
With a mantle it snares me.

My heart it's in pain
Because of this passion,
And I'm sleeping no better
Than a man in a prison.

Don't hold the candle of love
In your hand without lighting,
Banish all of the sadness
From my world in waiting.

Penalty Points

Ramps and penalty points,
Surmounting and genuflecting;
The powers that be
Roadside stopping; saying sorry
For being in a hurry,
Never realising its there
On the good stretches of road
They'll take you down to size,
Be you a Merc or Morris Minor.
You survived one of the old Mallow road types
Never ending double white lines
With some demon from hell, to you,
Hogging the road around thirty
If you're lucky, or less,
Maybe fifteen or twenty
If the load is large;
Or God forbid a tractor!
Or maybe you gave ten minutes of reflection
Waiting at faulty lights for road repairs.
So now with relief you settle in behind the wheel
To something from the sixties,
Tuning in the radio too.
Right foot slowly sinks!
Hit the road, hit the target!
Not so fast, a trap has sprung,
'I've been waiting for you'
That voice that purrs
As a bear snaps at the leaping salmon
On the river rapids -
"I'm in no hurry"
"What's the name sir?"
Some who drive and drink and drug

Some who drive and overtake - anywhere!
Criminals drive cars so -
'All drivers are criminals'
"Catch them at random
No time for fancy fishing"
"Just use a net and catch 'em all"
Ramps and penalty points,
Bow down and genuflect,
Dip your bonnet!
Oh, here we go again -
Pull in and plead your innocence.
"What speed do you think you were doing?
Pull in there - what's your name?"

Deadlines

Wrist watch spending
Currency of gold,
Life's best moments
So soon to go.

Left hand label,
Whip in hand,
Deadlines to death
From Creators breath.

Recall in cosmos
Time birth then -
Source of racing flow;
Run river, run free.

L'Aube d'Avril

Comme un très bon vin versés
D'une belle bouteille en verre,
Elle a dansée de tout coeur
En charmante ses partenaires
Avec sa gaieté musicale,
Compagnie désirée de la nuit
Au bon matin, une soirée,
Enchantante dans l'aube d'Avril,
En vue de voiliers aux quais.

Après, le goulot de la route
M'a avalé mil en mil,
Avec cette memoire dans la tête,
Dans le ventre de ma vie.

The April Dawn

Like a good wine poured
From a shapely bottle,
Joyful and charming,
Dancing with gaiety;
Amusing and musical
From head to toe,
Company of the night
To the early morning.
April dawn on the quays,
Sailing boats in the breeze.

Afterwards the road's bottleneck
Swallowed me up mile by mile:
All the memories in my head,
In the belly of my life.

Ode to a Sausage

Oh sausage, you're so spicy,
You're a sin!
It's not your body that excites me -
It's your skin.
You're so tanned and palpitating
On the pan, you're meant for eating,
As you sizzle on all sides
To be taken and be tasted,
To satisfy hunger
In a hot exciting way.

So hungry hounds who treat you
As just another sausage
On the way to satisfaction
Reflect and value better
The work of art you're eating!
Take your time before
You take another one.

West Clare

The mists and colours merge
In Clare the land of music;
See o'er the Cliffs of Moher
The sheer beauty far below,
Where the white surf agitated
Flies like seagulls in the air.
From The Falls to Doolin village,
To the bodhrán's easy beating
For the banjo and the fiddle
In O'Connor's famous pub;
Seated easy on a súgán
Is the gentle Micho Russell
And he's playing on the whistle
His own sweet tune *An Páistín Fionn*.
See the Burren, sort of moonface,
With it's rocks and Alpine flowers,
Take the road that leads to Poll na Brón.
Dolmen land of hidden rivers
Secret caves and limestone hillsides,
You're as lovely as a lady
Whose floral skirt is flouncing
Her flamenco to the sea.

Black Gloves

As a king to his throne
By the lake's bristling air,
I walked from the town
With the Queen of the Fair.

I held her gloved hand
As we sat by the shore,
And the peace of the land
Lay around my heart's core.

Fancy a cloud
So white and so pure,
Dream you're aboard
In the sky's blue azure.

Black gloves and white light
Was my vision so rare,
That the years of "what might?"
Seem too many to bear.

And whenever I'm lonely
And the world's not too good,
I think on her only
And the moon, lake and wood.

Tarbert

Tarbert and the curlew's call
O'er the Shannon arm
Stretching inland soothingly
Towards our dreams and reflections.
On near bank a man walks alone,
Stands, walks and looks again.

Birds together wheel in ecstasy
Over the waters of healing help
To all who care to stand apart
And see their souls.

It is evening-it is blessed!
Birdsong will die yet lingers.
Though ripples mar the water's mirror
Praise and incense rise to heaven
While here we stand
Till cold night drives us on.

On Waves of Love

Alone with God and Nature,
One few moments of spiritual peace
From the interchange of daily life.
This is how it can be
When our long day is past
And we move into the eternal Light.
Oh God! Is it worth it all
To love and not to be loved?
Yet, we must journey deep and deep
And hope to find content and peace.
Just now He sends the light of sun
To cheer the broken hearted lonely one.

I have waited much too long
And the hopes I had of seeing her
Are like the hopes of many
Such as I, such as have loved,
Once more dashed against the rocks!
And I am thrown once more
Upon the sands of aching hearts,
To be the loneliest one of all.
My dream has gone to stay awhile
But her smiling eyes still haunt my life.
Yes, shine on sun thou doest well
To make us think on heaven not on hell.

Exiled in Aldershot

By McAlpine's workers' hostel
The tall trees form a shade
From the evening's sultry sun
For the house and garden,
Where the children play.

The scene stirs memories
Of home at eve around the house
Playing 'hide and seek' together!
Then the world was far away -
Too far away to quench the joy
Unbroken still by life.

The man who keeps unto himself,
In the hostel that's his home,
Walks by and stops
And stoops to pat the friendly dog -
In this arid world of souls.

Star Flight

I was fast approaching land again,
My sails full blown, things all aright,
When then my blood ran cold within,
My star had vanished to leave dark night.

Who among men does not need a star -
A guide through life, faith hope and love?
Some stars are dim, their distance far,
My star was bright and reigned above.

Some stars are now of late discovered,
But my star has always been my light,
From tender age when feelings recovered
To blossom forth, to begin the fight.

A fight for what, why make a fight?
But a fight I made and the fight lasts still,
That star I fought for lest others might
Draw on my footsteps and claim my will.

The seas ran high, my boat astride,
I lost my star, things dark and dim
Pressed on my mind, the boat sailed wide,
No sight of land, no hope within.

Sail on, sail straight to a happy goal
If you have a star, a star of love,
And I will wait for clouds to clear,
Perhaps revealing sweet peace, sweet dove.

Gap in the Wind

There's a gap in the strange sí -gaoithe,
A storm that's brewing all day,
It's the grief and the sorrow we're feeling
For the loss of our laoch gone away?
The eyes of the big bridge are looking
As nature is circling so cold
To bear him, John B, to the places
He had strolled in the evenings of old.
Blowing by beech, oak and hazel
That stand in attention for him,
There they bow their high heads to the hero
In farewell to the man who loved them.
The wind that's now gone up the river
For the sake of John B's final tour
Will take him straight home to his heaven
Following the Feale as it blows -
He'd loved its sweet voice for a lifetime
Now his peacemaker sees him ashore.

The Driver

As on the train we ran
On the railway line so smooth
We ironed out our feelings
Within the fabric of our lives.
No need for fears or tears,
The driver is so skillful
In the art of shepherding his flock
To their final destinations.
He's up there for all our sakes
Like God sits in the heavens.
His Tralee train is Heuston bound,
On iron wheels so strong,
To bring us all tonight to Dublin.

Pierced

Grey skies beyond o'er Kerry Head
Half hide another summer sunset;
Soft shades of damson and damask
So full of evening expectations.

Far above the Kilflynn fields
A slit of brightness breaks,
Releasing slanted rays of light,
Like water from the side of Christ.

The Strength of Love

Leave the lake, the cove, the pond,
Open seas call glittering from beyond;
Depth and beauty lie there all awaiting,
Take the wheel for fear of hesitating.

Dig not earth that's only inches deep,
Nor sail in water where the willows weep -
Rocky ground no riches can possess,
Shallow waters yield no more or less.

Man is hemmed in by the world,
Give him space his spirit spreads unfurled;
Give him love, his battle-axe for clearing
The path of life of snares to space appearing.

Battle-axe resist not my faint grasping,
"Yes, my master, magic ways for you I'm asking",
"Rest now my human traveller I'm for you,
I'll make you sunlit paths from here to Xanadu".

Lá Márta

Clog ag bualadh go rialta;
Meán lae i gCill Áirne
I gciúnas an chlochair,
An ghrian ag fógairt an Earraigh.
Flaithiúlacht na mban rialta
Maidin chúrsa insheirbhíse,
Caife is caint chneasta,
Léachtóirí ar a ndícheall.
I bhfaid uainn an bás-
Snip na sreangán saolta;
Clog ag bualadh mall brónach
Don mharbh i mBéal Átha Longphoirt -
Eamy Walsh á thabhairt chun cille,
Comhairleoir Contae ciúin uasal,
Ciarraíoch na gcéadta cairde
A anam thar Sionainn in airde.

March Day

Regular beat of a bell
At Angelus time in Killarney
For the convent community,
So filled with peace
In the sunshine of Spring.
Kindly nuns so good to us
With tea and chat for teachers
On the morning of our course
Where the speakers were supreme .
Faraway a death,
Slender thread of life snipped.
The slow bell sounding
For the dead in Bally -
Eamy Walshe being buried;
County Councillor quiet and calm
Kerryman of many friends,
His soul ascends o'er the Shannon.

Ears of Oats

To the river's edge I ran
To catch the grazing pony,
Gave him ears of oats,
Put on his leather bridle.
We ambled to the water
To see the tall bulrushes,
Plucked one and held it up,
King in my own kingdom.

High Tide

White light of rain
On ash trees green and gold,
Roses red and wild beneath.
Thoughts on death but time for life,
I hear the cry of a child.

Galway shops were busy.
Not so everyone -
There was a man
Who stood alone
Observing.

Thoughts on family things;
Crying of the wind -
But love beats loneliness.

On a pencil hill
Miles away
Our house looks out
With vacant stare
On Kerry North -
My destiny to the sea.

The tide tonight
Was glued to Oranmore,
In the fullness of its savagery -
Always raw even in July.

A Wandering Spirit

To stay at home and not to wander,
Which is best I oft-times ponder -
The Aughtys in front and the Pins behind
And in between priceless peace of mind.

What beauty lies in other lands,
What can be done with my two hands?
These thoughts oft to my mind occur
When I am reasoning what God made me for.

It's not that I have not travelled beyond
The shores of my country and sireland fond,
For two summers past I regret to say
It has been my lot to sail faraway.

We travel far and live in many places,
We work our day with downcast faces,
Return home to a place of habitation
Which to many means dissipation.

When evening's light is gently fading
We stroll in parks our memories parading,
The full moon's face casts a look of pity
On a lonely emigrant in an unfriendly city.

Matt Mooney (2003)

Cailín an Lomaire Faiche

Chugam is uaim,
Anonn is anall,
Iníon na gréine -
Lomnocht a géaga
I leisce an lae
Lena lomaire faiche;
Cumhra an fhéir,
Brothall na Bealtaine.

The Lawn-mower Lady

To me and away,
To and fro,
Sun girl waltzing
With her lawnmower -
Bare limbed
In the lazy afternoon.
Scent of grass
In the month of May.

The Worker Bee

God sends the bee to cheer the mind
When life to me seems dull and blind,
The small wee thing with a sweet refrain
Elevates my spirit to a higher plain.

More pleasant than our chanticleer
The bee banishes doubt and fear,
Humming with industry and proud content
He gladdens my heart, he's heaven sent.

He is sure of his part in nature's plan
Which has been fixed by God for man.
He seeks not reasons why he should toil -
He's too busy with honey all the while.

Concerto

How happy the man
At the end of his sleeping
To hear the call of a robin
While the baby's awaking;
Then love sweeps away
All the dregs of the darkness
As she leaps to his arms,
To her father's embraces.

Autumn Gifts

It is autumn, yet I feel no loss
As one feels when summer's heat is gone.
With green fields, the smell of hay,
Birdsong and the brightness of air,
That brings images of foreign lands,
Steeped in the tropic sun.
This lightness that brings
Light feelings and delight
And a sense of pleasure
To happy human hearts.

Yet, they know long summer's day will pass
To wing in sober autumn
And frozen winter;
But still will feel,
When it has gone
The thrills and glorious feelings felt
With friends of gaiety
In hours of rapture
Beneath the sun on golden beaches
Bereft of pain.

Or beneath the celestial moon
On summer nights now gone,
When all heaven poured down
To fill two hearts with love to last
Though seasons change and chide.
Yes, autumn to me is a banner of hope,
A glowing ripe pear -
Fresh feelings I cannot define.

Even though the winter's reign
Will soon be ruling all
And already it's breath
Is cooling autumnal air,
It is a time of quietness
Certain things are won -
Rewards of labour's lost
On spring and summer fields;
And what's the use of spring
If autumn yields not fruit?

Autumn's store of gilded gifts
To me has given
A prize deprived of,
Long desired and loved.
Greetings my friend,
For some you end
A season of happy hours,
For me -
I see once more
The beauty in flowers.

In step

Arm in arm the old pair pass
By St. Johns, The Square, together;
Step by step, its clear they've loved
Through all the kinds of weather.

Humpty Dumpty' Eile

Gnáth imreas an lae
A spreag splancaí na feirge,
Lasta go tobann le cráiteacht
A thuirling ar mhuin an lanúin.
Tinneas an toist ar leathadh,
Buillí tolla a chroí sa tigh,
Ó sheomra go seomra, ag dúnadh dóirse.
Cailín ceithre bliana beo mar bhláth faoi chos
Ard glór na bruíne á tiomáint
Ina haonar go seomra na mbréagán,
Fothain ón stoirm á lorg.
Sheasas ag a doras is dfhéachas isteach -
I ina suí ar an urlár ag athrá a rann
I nguth caoin ón a croí gan smál -
"Humpty Dumpty sat on the wall."

Hawthorns

Hawthorn dreams, one pink, one white,
Once seen from an ivied bridge
Arched in stone o'er the river bed
Where the shining otters play -
Shy and black, their secrets dark
They take in their flight from me.
Scent of blossoms now I smell,
Though bleak the sky grey scene
Across the woods of Gurtinard,
Where trees stand bare and still
Against the rain that hides the hill,
The *Ides of March today.*

Little Hands

There is so much love to know
In the touch of your baby's hand,
There's a power with a warm flow
Like a wave on the silken sand.

Another Humpty Dumpty

The tensions of twosomeness
Set off the sparks
That suddenly flared
Into angry fires
Descending on their lives.
The sickly silence spread
With hollow heart
From room to room.
Put underfoot a flower,
A four year old
Little girl blown away
By the sound of the storm,
Alone with her dolls
In her air raid shelter.
From her bedroom door
I saw her seated there
Saying over and over
Her rhyme of the fall
Of Humpty Dumpty
Who sat on the wall.

Pearl

Blending with the pale pink
Of the cherry blossom bloom
For a short while in the Square,
Framed by the brevity of beauty
You were a fresh pearl there,
An argument against despair.